LSR A
Stage 4

RACE TO THE SOUTH POLE

Lewis Jones and Bernard Brett

Longman

Longman Group UK Limited
Longman House, Burnt Mill, Harlow,
Essex CM20 2JE, England
and Associated Companies throughout the world.

First published 1976
Ninth impression 1987

Acknowledgements
We are grateful to the following for permission to reproduce copyright material:

Museum of Modern Art for page 1; Royal Norwegian Embassy for page 2; Paul Popper Ltd for pages 3, 5, 8, 9, 14/15, 16 top and bottom, 17, 20; Scott Polar Research Institute for pages 6/7, 10, 11, 18, 19, 22/23, 28/29; John Murray (Publishers) Ltd for pages 12/13; The Cavalry Club for page 26/27; The Mansell Collection for page 30.

Note
The drawings and paintings on pages 6, 11, 18/19, 22/23, 28/29 were made by Wilson on an earlier visit to the Antarctic. They are now in the Scott Polar Research Institute, Cambridge.

Produced by Longman Group (FE) Ltd
Printed in Hong Kong

ISBN 0-582-53848-3

RACE TO THE SOUTH POLE

How it began:

In September 1909 the Englishman Robert Scott bought the ship *Terra Nova.* He had decided to reach the South Pole before anyone else. In that same month the Norwegian Roald Amundsen was fixing his own ship, the *Fram.* He was getting ready to go to the North Pole.

Then the world received a message from the Arctic: the American, Peary, had reached the North Pole. Amundsen, thought again. When Scott reached Australia, a telegram was waiting for him: 'Madeira. Am going South. *AMUNDSEN.*'

The race had begun.

Both men made camp in the Antarctic, but Amundsen's camp was 100 kilometres nearer to the Pole than Scott's.

The two men had different ideas about the journey. SCOTT: 'I am not sure about the dogs, but the ponies are going to be good. Ponies and men pulling—these are the best answers to the problem.'

Scott's ship the Terra Nova

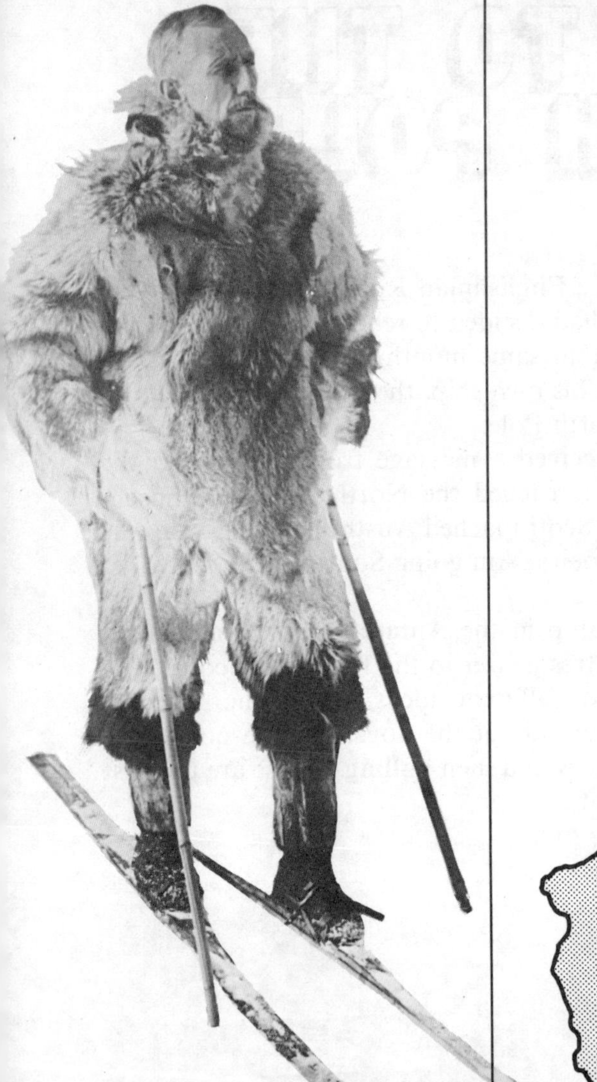

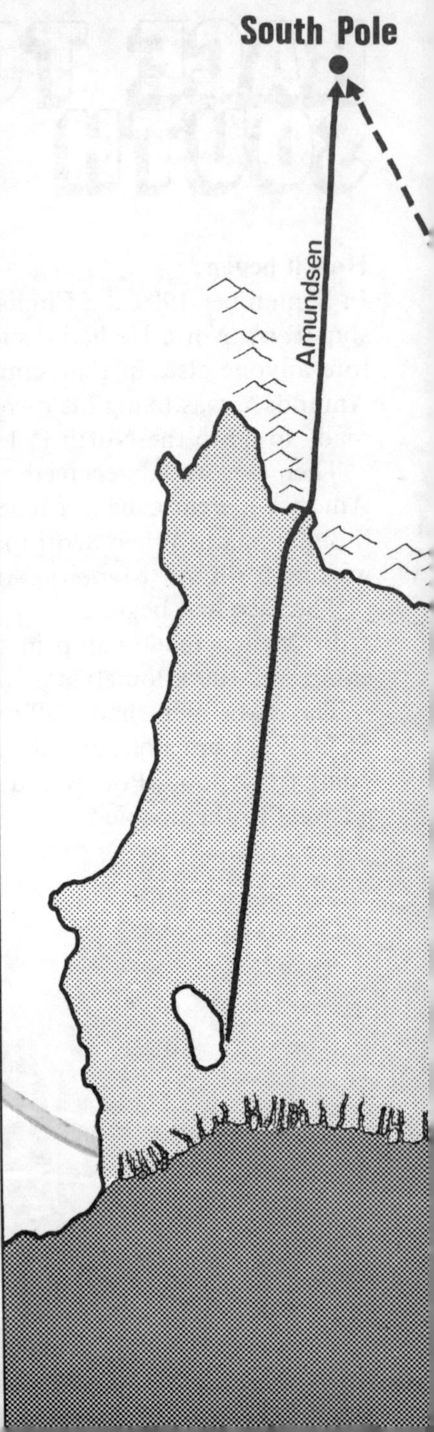

Amundsen

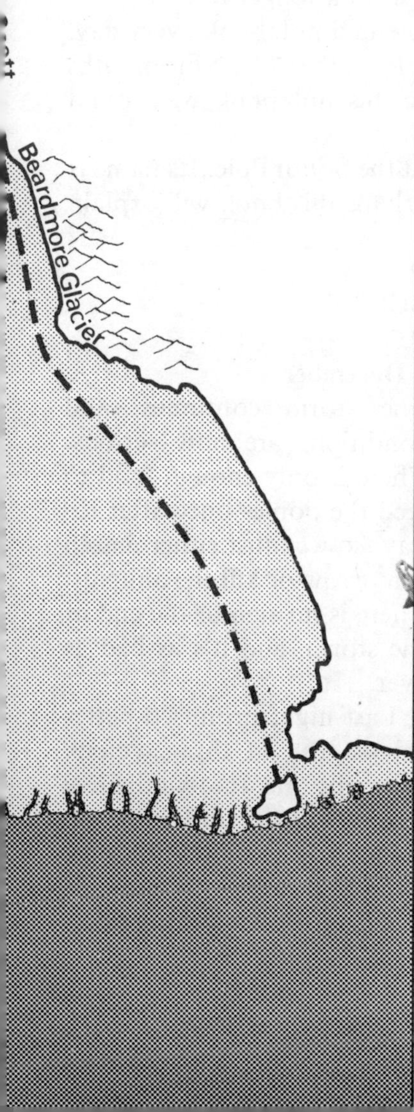

Scott

AMUNDSEN: 'Ponies? A great mistake. Dogs are the best animals in snow and ice. There are 22 kilos of food in the body of an Eskimo dog . . .'

There were five men in Amundsen's group. At first there were four in Scott's group. But after the Beardmore Glacier, he suddenly decided to have five—Scott, Bowers, Evans, Oates, and Wilson. But there were only four pairs of skis, so one man always had to walk without any. There was not enough proper food for five, and it took longer to cook.

Both Amundsen and Scott wrote in a notebook every day. Amundsen brought his book back from the Pole. Nine months after Scott died in the Antarctic, his notebook was found beside his body in the tent.

Today a modern camp stands at the South Pole. Its name is the Scott-Amundsen Station—perhaps this book will explain why.

AMUNDSEN

7 December

I cannot tell you my feelings at this moment. All the sledges stopped, and above the one in front the Norwegian flag was flying. It hung free, and danced in the air with soft sounds of comfort. It looked wonderfully well in the clean air and the shining whiteness all around. 88°23′ was past; we were further south than anyone before us. No other moment in the trip gave me as much pleasure as this. I was so happy that I cried; I could not stop myself.

. . . We were all pleased and excited; we had come far because we had worked well together. But our plan was to go

SCOTT

7 December

The storm continues, and conditions are now serious. There is only enough food to feed the ponies once after today; so we must either march tomorrow or kill the animals. There is no sign of the end of the storm, and it's as bad as ever.

Last night promised better things. But at three o'clock this morning the wind grew stronger again, and things returned to the old conditions. I can find no sign of an end; we all agree that it is not poss-

even further—to the end.

. . . Now there was almost no wind at all; it was bright and clear, like a true summer day. . . . . . . Wisty, Hansen and I were in worst condition after the last south-east storm. The left side of our faces had broken open; they were raw and wet. This was a great trouble to us in the last part of the trip. The smallest breath of wind hurt badly. It felt like a heavy knife cutting backwards and forwards across the face.

ible to move. We must just wait, and try not to be too unhappy. But it is not easy.

Our plans are surely worth more than this. They were properly made, and at first they served us well. No plan would be changed if we did it all again. We allowed enough time for bad weather—nobody could quarrel with that. But this December of storms—usually our finest month—has been a complete surprise. Not even the most careful plans could include conditions like this. It is terrible to

Scott with one of the ponies pulling a sledge. The ponies, and men like Meares (see page 7) in the support party, came on the first part of the journey. They made depots of food and oil for Scott's return journey, and then the support party went back.

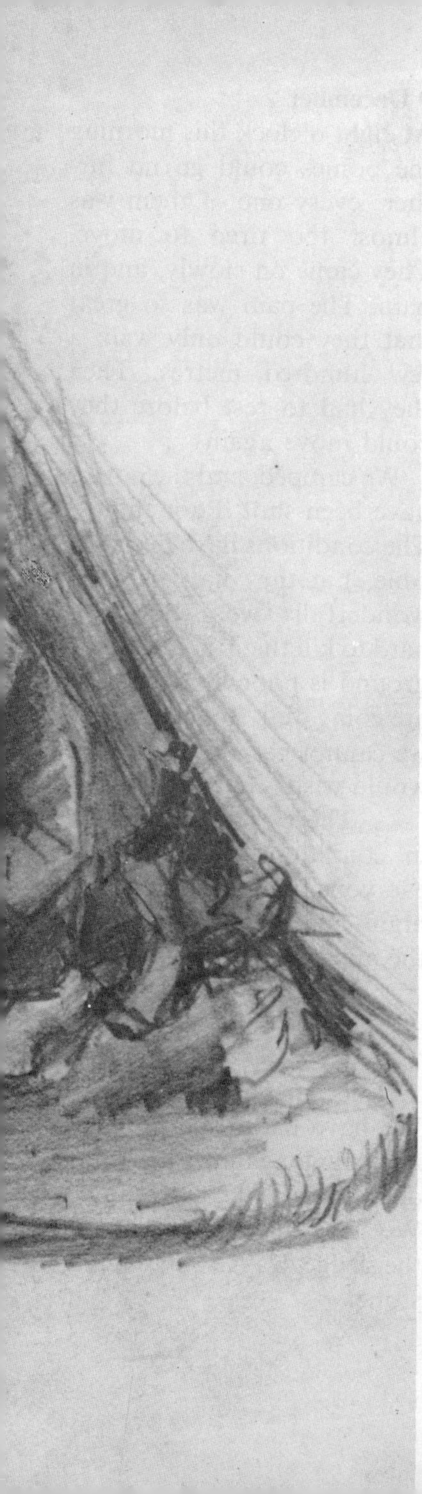

lie here in a wet sleeping-bag, and think of the fears and the difficulties . . .

Things go from bad to worse. The shining brightness of the snow has attacked Meares' eyes terribly: now he cannot see out of one eye . . . There cannot be many happy hearts in the camp in weather like this. But there is hope—last night I heard someone laughing.

. . . I sit here and watch the wet green walls of our tent; the shining wet wood of the tent-poles; the cold clothes hanging in the middle, heavy with water; the sad faces of my friends. I listen to the snow dancing across the tent every minute of the day; and the wind busily fingering the tent-cloth. My clothes are just cloth and water. Everything I touch is wet. And I know that outside there is only a great wall of whiteness all around—this is our only home. And we are wondering now if all our plans will fail. No one could wish to be in these conditions. But still we can go on trying. Perhaps these difficulties will even give us courage.

9 December
Every step we now took brought us quickly nearer to the Pole; we were almost certain to reach it on the afternoon of the 14th... What would we see when we got there? A great flat white desert without end; a land that no eye had yet seen; a land where no foot had yet stood. But perhaps —no, it was not possible. We had travelled so fast that we must reach the Pole first... But no one can be *completely* sure. And when a man is not sure, he is attacked by dark thoughts and wild fears.

9 December
At eight o'clock this morning the ponies could go no further: every one of them was almost too tired to move. They came on slowly, and in pain. The pain was so great that they could only walk a few hundred metres. Then they had to rest before they could move again...

We camped, and the ponies have been shot. Poor things! The conditions have been terrible, but they have worked wonderfully well. But it is hard to kill them so early. The ground is poor, but the dogs are going well. But here again, we cannot get all the help we would wish.

...There is little pleasure in conditions like this. But everyone seems happier tonight, and there is laughter in the air.

12 December
We are travelling fast. Ground as good as ever. Weather wonderful—sunshine and no wind.

12 December
We have had a hard day... Again and again we drop into deep snow and cannot move. We used all our power, but the sledge dragged like a great stone.

13 December
The weather in the morning had been just as fine as before; in the afternoon we had some snow from the south-east. We were all excited that night in the tent. It was like the night before some great ceremony. We knew that a great day was near.

13 December
A hard and *terrible* day. We started at eight—the pulling was terribly difficult. I do not think we have gone more than seven kilometres today; and our hopes have changed very little.

We can only continue pulling, but there is little cause for happiness. I am not at all hungry, but quite thirsty. Two sea-birds came round the camp at noon. I am sure our 'Shambles' camp drew them to us. (The camp where the ponies were shot.)

14 December
On the morning of December 14th, the weather was of the finest—a beautiful day to arrive at the Pole.

. . . At three in the afternoon the cry, 'Stop!' rang out from all the drivers. The sledges had meters to measure distance. The drivers were watching these carefully, and now all the meters showed full distance—the Pole! The South Pole was reached—the trip ended.

. . . After this came the greatest and most important act of the trip—the planting of our flag. Love and duty shone in five pairs of eyes that looked upon the flag. It unwound itself with a loud sound like a gun, and rode the wind above the Pole.

Of course there was excited laughter in the tent that evening. It's not that bottles were opened and drinks were flowing—no, we each had to be happy with a little piece of meat. Everything with us now had to be marked with the words 'South Pole' and the date.

. . . Inside the tent, in a little bag, I left a letter to the King. It told him of our trip and its happy ending. I also wrote a short letter to Captain Scott—I believed he would be the first to find the tent.

Left
Amundsen at the Pole

14 December
I was kept awake for some time last night. The food I had eaten was giving me pain; and my clothes were full of water. The very hard exercise is causing pains all over our bodies. Our mouths are getting raw, and painful to touch. I am glad to say that everyone's eyes are getting better. We are just starting our march, but we do not have great hopes. (Temperature $-10.5°C$, $+13°F$)

Evening . . . Near the end of our march, we were pulling our loads very easily. It is wonderful to be moving so well. At last we are seeing some results for all our hard work.

24 December
The day before Christmas. The weather was changing rather a lot—now grey, now clear. Wisty was cook for the day. He put all the biscuit crumbs into a bag, he took this into the tent, and then broke the biscuit crumbs into even smaller pieces. He pushed the bag and pulled it, and turned it over and over... Then he mixed in a sausage of dried milk. With these, Wisty made a very good dish of Christmas porridge. We all smoked one of Bjaaland's cigars, and the day felt like a holiday.

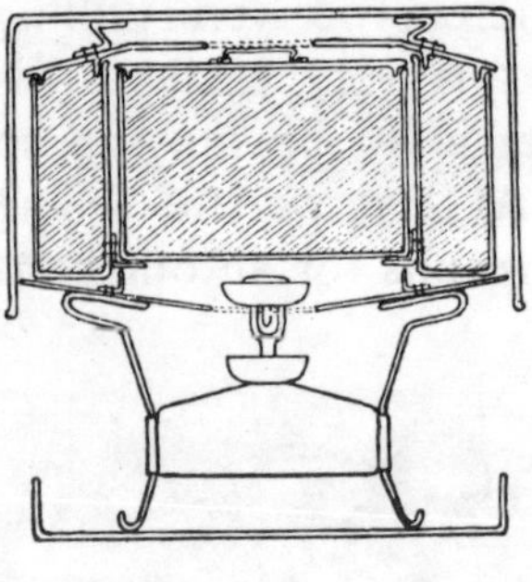

They cooked on a stove like this.

24 December
(Temperature -19.4°C, -3°F)
We have only one real trouble —ice continues to form on our faces. The temperature is never far from zero... We are quite happy today. Tomorrow is Christmas Day, with something special to eat and drink.

25 December
(Temperature -21.5°C, -7°F)
Keeping away from deep holes in the snow and ice; and travelling a little downhill. We have come along quite quickly—wonderful.

I must write a few words of our meal last night. We had four dishes. The first, pemmican—and plenty of it!—with slices of horse meat, and onion and curry-powder. We mixed in biscuits to make it thick. Then some cocoa and biscuit, mixed into a sweet soup. Then a plum pudding. Then cocoa with raisins. And lastly, a sweet dish of caramels and ginger. After the

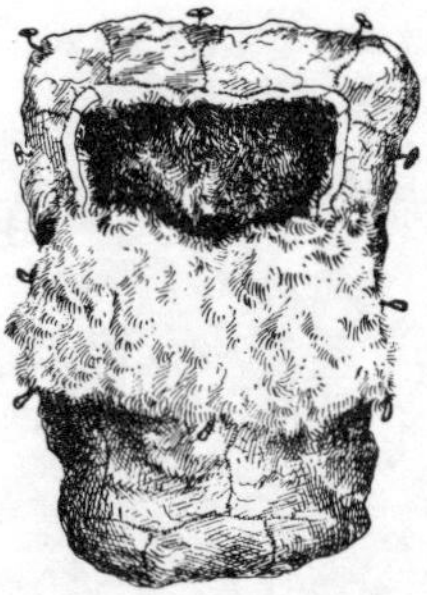

13 January
We believed we would reach the depot in 83°S. It was not a very good day to find the depot. There was no wind, and a fog came up. The fog was so thick that we could only see a few metres in front of us.

...Then there was a clear space in the thick wall of fog. And there—not many metres away—was our depot.

16 January
We allowed ourselves a rather good meal here in 82. I still clearly remember the sweet taste of Wisting's 'Chocolate Pudding'—I may uncover the secret of this dish for you. Take biscuit crumbs and dried milk and chocolate. Put them all into hot water. What happens next? I don't know. For the rest of the secret, ask Wisting.

meal it was difficult to move. Wilson and I couldn't finish our plum pudding. We have all slept very well indeed, and we felt beautifully warm. Three cheers for good food!

13 January
(Temperature -30°C, -22.5°F) ... Only 80 kilometres from the Pole tonight. If we don't get to it, we will be very close indeed. There is a light south wind tonight: I very much hope it will grow stronger.

16 January
(Temperature -30.8°C, -23.5° F)... The worst has happened, or almost the worst. By noon we had reached 89°42′S; and we started off again full of life in the afternoon. We believed that tomorrow we would see the Pole. Bowers has good eyes, and after two hour's march he saw something. He thought it was a pile of stones. He was not too pleased... We marched on, and we reached it. It was a black flag; and

Scott and his men find Amundsen's tent near the Pole.

it was tied to a long piece of wood from a sledge. Near it there were signs of a camp; the marks of sledges in the snow; marks of skis that had come and gone again; and the clear signs of the feet of dogs —many dogs. This told us the complete story. The Norwegians have been here before us, and they were first at the Pole. It is a terribly sad thought, and I am very sorry for my good friends...

Tomorrow we must march on to the Pole; and then we must hurry home as fast as we can. All dreams must go; it will be a cruelly hard return. Certainly we are going downhill—certainly also the Norwegians found an easy way up.

17 January

(Temperature -30°C, -22°F at start. Night -29.4°C, -21°F) The Pole. Yes, but we did not believe the end of our trip would be like this. We have had a bad day... We started at 7.30. None of us slept much after the surprise of our discovery... Great God! This is a terrible place. We have worked so hard and so long

18 January
Unusually fine weather today. The ground is very difficult—holes and hills and valleys all around... Great pieces of ground have fallen away, and the most terrible holes have opened—big enough to destroy many groups like ours. Hansen went halfway into one of these holes. But I'm glad to say he got out again without difficulty.

Scott and his unhappy group at the Pole.

to get here. Now we do not even have the prize of being first. Well, it is something to get here at all... Still, we must not keep heavy hearts. We have had a thick Polar soup, and we feel comfortable inside... Now it is time for the run home. It will be a hard fight—I wonder if we can do it.

18 January
We have just arrived at this tent, 3 kilometres from our camp—so it is 2 km from the Pole. In the tent we find that five Norwegians have been here:

Roald Amundsen
Olav Olavson Bjaaland
Hilmer Hanssen
Sverre H Hassel
Oscar Wisting

16 Dec 1911

...There is a note from Amundsen. It asks me to send his letter to King Haakon. There were also some sleeping-bags, and some clothes. ...Well, we have turned our backs now on our prize, the Pole. Ahead of us now are 1300 km of heavy dragging. Goodbye to most of the dreams.

25 January
We reached our good little house again (Franheim), with two sledges and eleven dogs. Men and animals seemed happy and well.

We came in . . . one after another they woke up—'What about the Pole?'—'Have you been there?'—'Yes of course. Otherwise you wouldn't have seen us again.'

The trip has taken 99 days. Distance covered—3000 kilometres.

(The end of Amundsen's notes)

25 January
(Temperature -23.8°C, -11°F)
. . . Thank God we found our Half Degree Depot. Digging out the sledge was long and terribly cold work. But at last we packed the tents and began the march home. All pulling . . . We are not without troubles. Oates has a very cold foot; Evans' fingers and nose are in bad condition; and tonight Wilson has terrible pains in the eyes. Bowers and I are the only ones without troubles at the present . . . Snowstorms are our worst enemy. They not only stop our marches; but the cold, wet air makes the work very difficult.

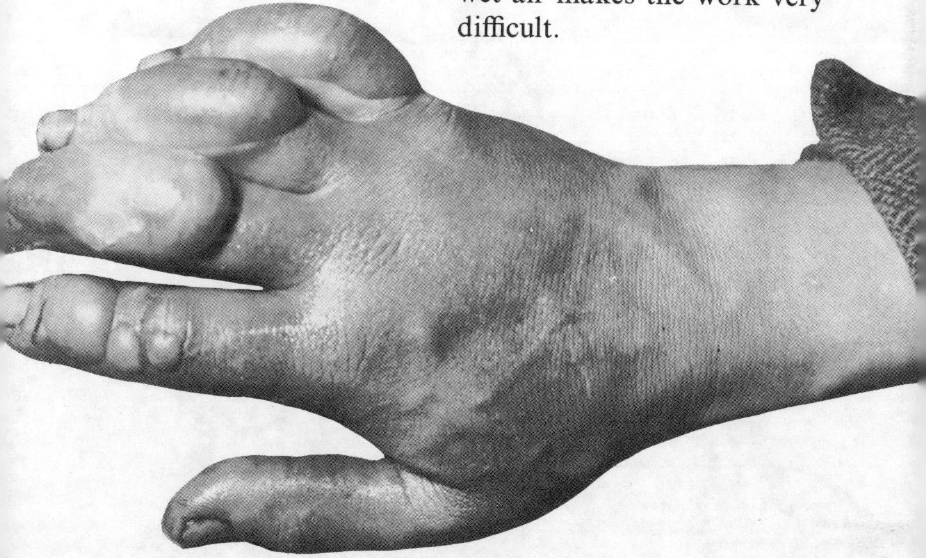

Some of Wilson's drawings of the men pulling the sledges.

17 February

A very terrible day. Evans looked a little better after a good sleep; he told us he was quite well. But he always says that. He started in his place, and began to pull the sledge. But half an hour later, his ski shoes were coming off, and he had to leave the sledge...

We stopped after an hour, and Evans came up again—but very slowly. Half an hour later he stopped again for the same reason. He tried to tie the shoe tight. I said he should come on as quickly as he could. He answered with something of a smile, I thought. We had to go ahead, and the rest of us had to pull very hard. Our clothes and our bodies got wetter. We stopped near Monument Rock. Evans was a long way behind, so I camped for a meal. There seemed to be no problem at first, so we made tea. Then we made our own meal, and ate it. After that, Evans had still not appeared. We looked out and saw him in the far distance. Now we recognised trouble, and all four started back on skis.

I was the first to reach the

Evans

poor man. When I saw him he was in a dangerous condition. He was on his knees, and some of his clothes were coming off. His hands were uncovered, and the cold had attacked them badly. There was a wild look in his eyes. We pulled him on to his feet; but after two or three steps he dropped down again. He lay on the ground and did not move. Wilson, Bowers and I went back for the sledge, while Oates remained with him. When we returned, Evans was not properly awake. And when we got him into the tent, his eyes were shut.

He died quietly at 12.30 at night... Wilson thinks he hurt his head in a fall. It is a terrible thing to see a friend die in this way.

2 March

Troubles do not often come alone. We marched quite easily yesterday afternoon. But since then, three things have made our conditions worse.

First, we found we did not have enough oil. We must use it with great care; but still I do not think there is enough to take us to the next depot (115 km away). Second, Titus Oates showed us his feet—the cold has attacked them, and the toes are very bad indeed. Our third piece of trouble came in the night. The wind has usually been a good friend to us; but this time it brought heavy clouds and dark grey skies... I am afraid we have great problems. We cannot march as far as we should; and we feel the cold terribly.

4 March

Things look *very* black indeed ... As usual, we forgot our troubles last night. We had some good soup; then we got into our bags and slept very well. When we woke up, we had more soup. Then we started marching. There will be little help for us now, except perhaps more food at the next depot. It will be bad if there is no oil there. Shall we get there?... If Wilson and Bowers were not so full of life, what would I do? I don't know.

Pulling a sledge in a snowstorm.

5 March
Going from bad to worse, I'm afraid...We went to bed after a cup of cocoa and some pemmican. (Pemmican free from ice, but still hard.) We are able to do less and less, and Oates is worst of all. His feet are in a terrible condition. ...Very little oil remains now, and the poor soldier (Oates) is almost finished. It is an unhappy time, because we can do nothing for him. More hot food might help a little—but only a little, I'm afraid. None of us thought this terrible cold could be so cruel. It is worse for Wilson than the rest of us. He is spending a lot of time and trouble on Oates' feet: these are in poor condition, and Wilson is always doctoring them...

Still, we shall continue with all our courage...We can only say, 'God help us,' and drag our tired feet forward. We are all cold and unhappy, but we try not to show it. We talk of all kinds of things in the tent—but not much of food. We have decided to continue with full meals. There are dangers of course; but we just couldn't remain hungry all this time.

6 March
This morning things have been terrible...Poor Oates is not able to pull...He is very brave indeed, since his feet must be hurting him badly...If we were all well and strong, I would hope to get back safely. But the poor soldier is now making us terribly slow. He does his best, but he is in great pain, I fear.

7 March
A little worse, I fear. One of Oates' feet *very* bad this morning...But I want to continue to the end, if possible.

8 March
Worse and worse in morning: poor Oates' left foot can never continue like this. Wilson's feet giving trouble now. (Mostly because he gives so much help to others.)...If we cannot get more oil, God help us indeed. But even without that problem, things are very bad for us now, I fear.

11 March

Titus Oates is very near the end, I think. What will we or he do? God only knows. We talked of these things after breakfast. He is a very brave fellow, and he understands the dangers. But he almost asked us for advice. There was not much to say. We could only advise, 'March for as long as you can.' One good result from this conversation: there are some things that can end a man's troubles for ever. Since Wilson is a doctor, he has some of these things. I told him to give them to us (it was almost an order). . . . We now each have 30 opium tablets, and we know how to use them.

16 or 17 March

Not sure of the date; but think the last correct. Things still getting worse. Two days ago, at noon, poor Titus Oates said he couldn't continue. He said we should leave him in his sleeping-bag. We could not do that, and we advised him to join the afternoon march. At night he was worse, and we knew that the end had come. If these words are found, I want the facts to be known. Oates' last thoughts were of his mother . . . Hope never left him before the end . . . There was a wild snowstorm. He said, 'I am just going outside. I may be some time.' He went out into the snowstorm, and we have not seen him since. We knew that poor Oates was walking away to die. We advised him to stay. But we knew it was the act of a brave man and an English gentleman. We all hope to meet the end with this kind of courage —and surely the end is not far away . . . We talk all the time of completing the trip. But I don't think any of us believes it in his heart.

19 March

We camped with difficulty last night. We were terribly cold before our meal—cold pemmican and biscuit, and half a pan of hot cocoa. Then —to our surprise—we got warm, and all slept well.

Sledge terribly heavy. We are 25 km from the depot, and we ought to get there in three

'He went out into the snowstorm and we have not seen him since.'

days. So slow! We have two days food, but less than a day's oil. All our feet are getting bad—Wilson's best; my right foot worst, left foot all right. There is no chance to rest our feet if we cannot get hot food into us. If we ever get back, the feet must be cut off. It is too late to save them now. But will the trouble reach other parts of the body? That is the unhappy question. The weather doesn't give us a chance. The wind from North to North-West, and -40°C, -40°F temperature today.

21 March
Only 18 km from the depot Monday night; had to stop all yesterday in bad snowstorm. Today very little hope. Wilson and Bowers going to depot for oil.

22 and 23 March
Snowstorm as bad as ever—Wilson and Bowers not able to start—tomorrow last chance. No oil and almost no food now—must be near the end. Have decided—we shall march for the depot and die while we walk.

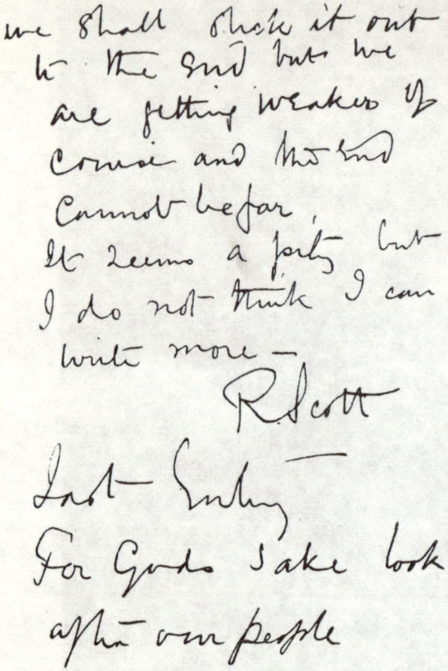

we shall stick it out
to the end but we
are getting weaker of
course and the end
cannot be far
It seems a pity but
I do not think I can
write more —
R Scott
Last Entry —
For Gods sake look
after our people

29 March

Since the 21st, a storm has continued from WSW and SW. We had oil to make two hot cups of tea each, and almost no food. Every day we have been ready to start for our depot (18 km away). But outside the wind rushes wildly all day, and the snow falls in thick piles against the tent . . . I do not think we can hope for any better things now. Our hearts will remain strong to the end. But our bodies are getting weaker of course, and the end cannot be far. It seems a pity, but I do not think I can write more.

R SCOTT

Last message.
For God's sake look after our people.